Teaching Healthy Cooking and Nutrition

in Primary Schools, Book 1

Fruit Salad, Rainbow Sticks, Bread Pizza and Other Recipes

Sandra Mulvany

Brilliant
PUBLICATIONS

We hope you and your pupils enjoy trying out the recipes in this book and learning about healthy eating. Brilliant Publications publishes many other books to help primary school teachers. To find out more details on all of our titles, including those listed below, please log onto our website: www.brilliantpublications.co.uk.

Other titles in the Teaching Healthy Cooking and Nutrition in Primary Schools series:

Other titles published by Brilliant Publications

Published by Brilliant Publications
Unit 10,
Sparrow Hall Farm,
Edlesborough,
Dunstable,
Bedfordshire,
LU6 2ES

www.brilliantpublications.co.uk

The name Brilliant Publications
and the logo are registered trade marks.

Written by Sandra Mulvany
Illustrated by Kerry Ingham
Cover design by Brilliant Publications
Photography by Brilliant Publications
Printed in the UK

© 2008 Sandra Mulvany (text); Brilliant Publications
(photography, design and layout)

Printed ISBN 978-1-78317-108-8
e-book ISBN 978-1-78317-114-9

The first edition of this book, published in 2008, had the
title: Healthy Cooking for Primary Schools, Book 1.
This second edition was first printed and published in
the UK in 2014

10 9 8 7 6 5 4 3 2 1

The right of Sandra Mulvany to be identified as the
author of this work has been asserted by herself in
accordance with the Copyright, Design and Patents Act
1988.

Contents

Lesson	Recipe	Teaching Point	Learning Objective	
1	Fruit Salad			13–18
		Skill	How to Cut	14
		Theory	Food and Us	15
		Health and Safety	Washing Your Hands	15
2	Rainbow Sticks			19–24
		Skill	How to Put Food on Skewers	20
		Theory	About Vitmin C	21
		Health and Safety	Cleaning Your Nails	21
3	Pitta Bread Filling			25–30
		Skill	How to Wash Fruit and Vegetables	26
		Theory	Why Wash Fruit and Vegetables?	27
		Health and Safety	Advantages of an Apron	27
4	Fruit Smoothie			31–36
		Skill	How to Remove Strawberry Stalks	32
		Theory	About Bananas	33
		Health and Safety	Using a Blender Safely	33
5	Bread Pizza			37–42
		Skill	How to Spread	38
		Theory	Where Does Flour Come From?	39
		Health and Safety	Reasons to Tie Back our Hair	39
6	Afternoon Tea Bread			43–48
		Skill	How to Weigh Ingredients	44
		Theory	Types of Flour – Which is Healthier?	45
		Health and Safety	Reasons to Avoid Dangly Sleeves	45

Contents (cont.)

Introduction and Links to the National Curriculum

The *Teaching Healthy Cooking and Nutrition in Primary Schools* series is a practical school programme for schools. It focuses on the progression in cooking skills through easy-to-follow recipes. Essential cooking skills, theory and health and safety points are introduced progressively throughout the series.

The programme is designed to teach pupils practical cooking whilst incorporating the theory into the hands-on activity. Each of the five books in the series contains 12 recipes, together with visual lesson structure cards, visual learning objectives and photographs of the food – all of which are photocopiable.

All the recipes are presented in two formats, one laid out in a traditional way and one in a visual step-by-step format, enabling the recipes to be used with pupils of all ages or with groups with differing reading abilities. It is recommended that, after a cooking session, the recipes are photocopied and sent home with pupils, so that children can try making the recipes at home.

There are two assessment sheets in the book (on pages 85–86). The assessment sheets test and reinforce the practical and theoretical knowledge gained. You will also find a photocopiable certificate on page 87 for when pupils have completed all the tasks.

This second edition of *Teaching Healthy Cooking and Nutrition in Primary Schools* has been amended to ensure that it addresses the requirements of the National Curriculum for England (September 2014). The programmes of study state that pupils should be taught how to cook and apply the principles of nutrition and healthy eating. It aims to instil in pupils a love of cooking and to teach them a life skill that will enable pupils to feed themselves and others affordably and well, now and in later life.

Key Stage 1 pupils should be taught to use the basic principles of a healthy and varied diet to prepare dishes and understand where food comes from.

Key Stage 2 pupils should be taught to:
* understand and apply the principles of a healthy and varied diet
* prepare and cook a variety of predominantly savoury dishes using a range of cooking techniques
* understand seasonality, and know where and how a variety of ingredients are grown, reared, caught and processed.

The series also links well with the Health and Wellbeing section of the Scottish Curriculum for Excellence and the Guidance on the Schools (Health Promotion and Nutrition) (Scotland) Act 2007.

How to Use the Resources

All ingredients are based on two pupils sharing, and the timings will all fit into a double lesson of approximately 80 minutes. We recommend you use low-fat options where possible.

Make a display using the Visual Lesson Structure Cards (pages 7–10) and pictures of the recipe and skill to be focussed on in the lesson (colour versions of the photographs can be downloaded from the Brilliant Publications' website).

Keep the skill, theory and health and safety point sheets to hand so that you can refer to them when demonstrating to pupils. (The language has been kept as simple as possible on these sheets, so you may wish to give copies to your pupils as well.)

Choose the best format of the recipe to use for each pair of children and photocopy sufficient copies. The illustrated versions of the recipes can be photocopied onto either an A3 sheet (if space is an issue, fold it in half so that you view six steps at a time), or reduced to A4 size.

If you place the recipes and other sheets in clear plastic wallets (or laminate them), they can be used again and again.

Encourage children to gather together all the ingredients and equipment they need before starting. They could tick things off on their copy of the recipe.

Demonstrate the recipe 2–3 steps at a time, introducing the skill, theory and health and safety points as you progress through the recipe.

An important aspect of learning to cook is learning to work together. You may wish to display the Discussion cards on pages 11–12 (Communicate, Share, Help, Be pleasant) so that you can refer to these throughout the lesson.

The assessment sheets on pages 85 and 86 provide a fun way of testing the practical and theoretical knowledge gained. The Certificate of Achievement on page 87 can either be used as an ongoing record or be given out when all the recipes in the book have been completed.

On pages 88–89 there is a chart giving some suggestions for adapting the recipes for children with allergies and intolerances, and/or religious and lifestyle considerations. None of the recipes use nuts. Before you start any cooking activities, you should send home a letter asking parents to inform you if there are any allergy/lifestyle/religious considerations that you need to take into account. You may need to follow this up with a letter or phone call to clarify any issues raised. A useful chart listing some religious food customs can be found at: www.childrensfoodtrust.org.uk/assets/the-standards/3food-customs.pdf.

Above all, have fun and enjoy cooking!

Today We are Making

1

Today We are Learning

2

Teaching Healthy Cooking and Nutrition, Book 1

Read Recipe

3

Healthy Cooking Recipe Book

Wash Hands and Prepare

4

Cook

5

Clear Away

6

Tasting

7

We Have Learnt

8

Communicate

It is vital to have good communication in a cooking environment. If you are working with a partner, it is important to say what you are doing and to agree on who does what. You have to talk about what you would like to do and listen to what your partner wants to do. Then you have to work out a way to make it fair for both of you. You can only come to an agreement if you talk together!

You should also let others know if there are any dangers, such as you opening the oven or if water has been spilt on the floor. Talking is absolutely key to good cooking habits. The better you are at communicating, the better you are at cooking in a school environment.

Share

Good sharing follows on from good communicating. If you have communicated well, you will have reached a fair decision about sharing. Sharing works best when it has been done fairly and everyone is happy. Sharing is particularly difficult if it involves doing something really exciting or really boring. You have to imagine that the other person feels very much like yourself. This can be hard to imagine, but it is an important lesson to learn. Sharing is a lot easier when you talk together about things.

Help

It is important to be able to help others, but it is also important to accept help from others. Help is a two-way thing. If you are offering your help to someone else, it is important that you choose your words carefully. Be kind in giving your help, as it can be hard to accept help given with harsh words. If you have communicated well, you will be able to help each other well. If you are very capable, offer your help kindly, but also let others help you in return, even if it is to do with something you feel you might already know about.

Be pleasant

It is, in fact, very simple to be pleasant. Look at and listen to the person you are working with and notice something he or she does well. Then say something pleasant about that. You will soon discover that the more pleasant you are to people, the more pleasant they are back to you. You can also do something pleasant, like smile at a person or pat someone kindly on the back. Don't just wait for someone to be pleasant to you; try to be the first one to say or do something pleasant.

Fruit Salad

How to Cut

Knives are sharp and can cut you very easily. Always be careful when using a knife. If you touch the blade it can cut you. Always hold the knife by its handle and point the sharp blade down towards the table or cutting board. (If you wish, you can put a mark on the top of the knife to show you which edge of the blade is sharp.)

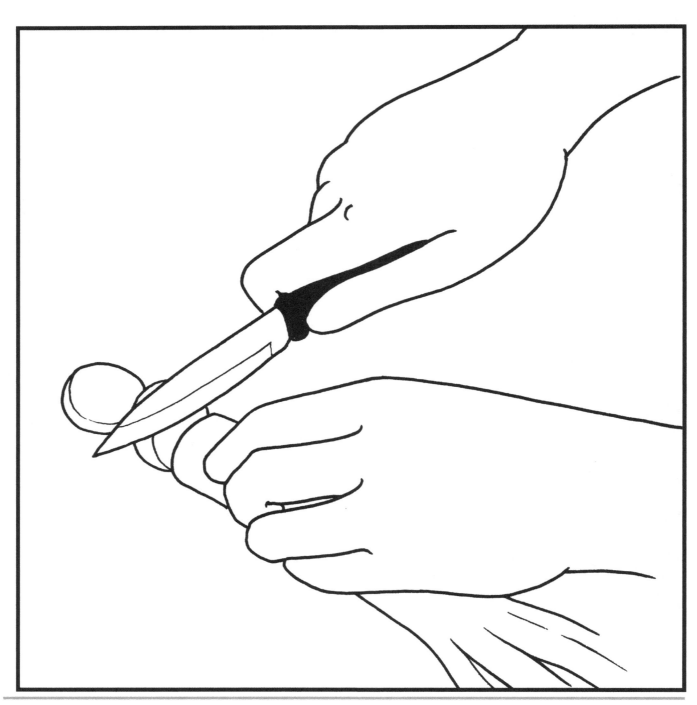

Food and Us

Food serves the same function for us as fuel does for cars. Without food and water we simply couldn't live. Food is full of nutrients (vitamins, minerals and proteins) that our body needs to work properly. There are different types of nutrients and these are found in different types of food. We need a little bit of all the different nutrients and that's why we have to eat a little bit of many different types of food. Food isn't just about keeping us from being hungry and filling us up. It is about getting all the right kinds of nutrients to make all the bits of our body work.

You may substitute the fruit suggested for fruit that is in season and grown locally. Look at the packaging to see from where the fruit originates. Find the places on a globe/world map.

Washing Your Hands

It is important to wash your hands before you start cooking. This is to wash off any dirt and bacteria. You have to wash your hands with warm water and soap. You should make your hands wet, add soap and then rub your soapy hands together away from the water for at least 20 seconds. Then rinse thoroughly under the water and dry your hands with a disposable towel.

Fruit Salad

Recipe

Ingredients:

Tin of peaches   Banana   Green grapes
Strawberries   Raspberries   Satsuma

1. Wash fresh fruit.

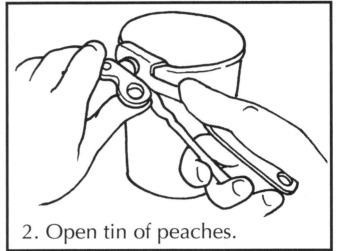

2. Open tin of peaches.

3. Sieve juice into bowl.

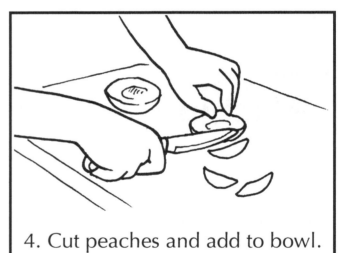

4. Cut peaches and add to bowl.

5. Peel and cut banana and add to bowl.

6. Cut grapes and add to bowl.

Fruit Salad (cont.)

Equipment:

Chopping board	Sharp knife	Tin opener
Bowl	Sieve	

7. Remove leafy stalks from strawberries by twisting them.

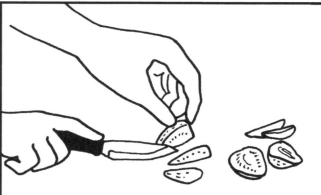

8. Cut strawberries and add to bowl.

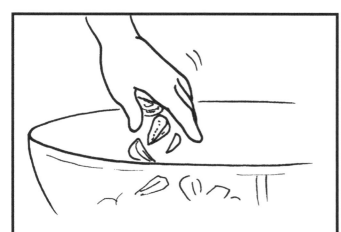

9. Add raspberries to bowl.

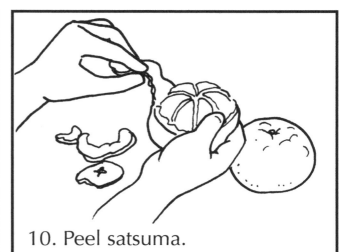

10. Peel satsuma.

11. Divide into segments and add to bowl.

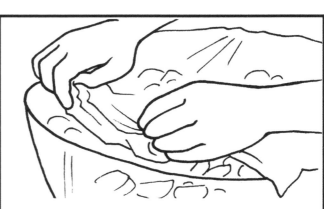

12. Cover fruit salad and keep cool in fridge.

Fruit Salad

Ingredients:
Tin of peaches
Banana
Green grapes
Strawberries
Raspberries
Satsuma

Equipment:
Chopping board
Sharp knife
Tin opener
Bowl
Sieve

Instructions:

1.   Wash fresh fruit.

2.   Open tin of peaches.

3.   Sieve juice into bowl.

4.   Cut peaches and add to bowl.

5.   Peel and cut banana and add to bowl.

6.   Cut grapes and add to bowl.

7.   Remove leafy stalks from strawberries by twisting them.

8.   Cut strawberries and add to bowl.

9.   Add raspberries to bowl.

10.   Peel satsuma.

11.   Divide into segments and add to bowl.

12.   Cover fruit salad and keep cool in fridge.

Rainbow Sticks

© Sandra Mulvany and Brilliant Publications

This page may be photocopied by the purchasing institution only.

Teaching Healthy Cooking and Nutrition, Book 1

www.brilliantpublications.co.uk   **19**

Skill

How to Put Food on Skewers

A skewer has one very sharp end. Therefore, be careful when you thread something onto a skewer. Hold the skewer carefully with one hand and hold the food between your fingers and thumb. Then thread the food on gently, making sure that the palm of your hand is to the side of the skewer.

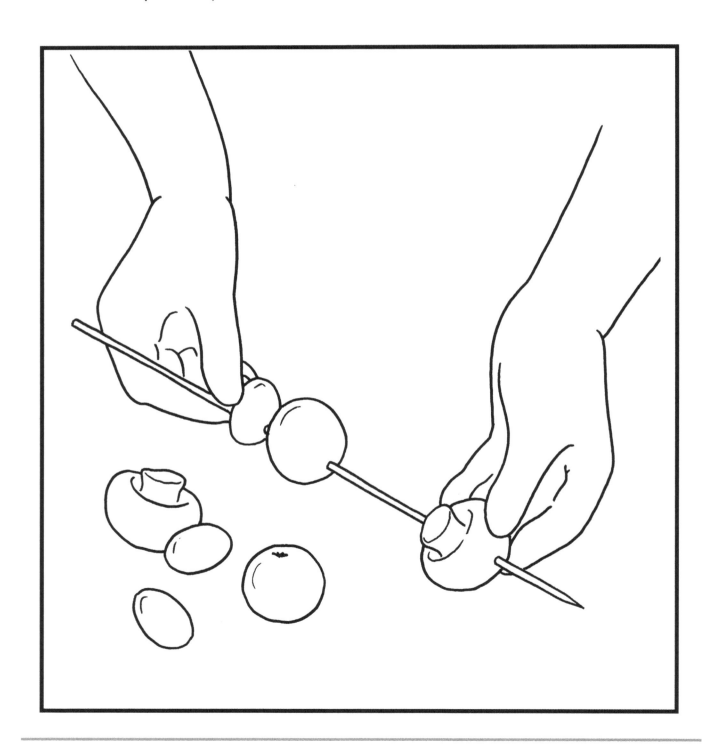

About Vitamin C

There are many types of vitamins, such as vitamins A, B, C, D, E and K. Vitamins are a type of nutrient which the body needs. Fruit and vegetables are excellent sources of all vitamins – especially vitamin C. Vitamin C plays a very important protective role in the body. Unlike most animals, humans cannot produce vitamin C, so we need it in our diet. Although we need only a small amount of vitamin C, we cannot store it in our bodies and so we have to eat food rich in vitamin C on a regular basis.

You may substitute the fruit and vegetables suggested for fruit and vegetables that are in season and grown locally. Look at the packaging to see from where the fruit and vegetables originate. Find the places on a globe/world map.

Cleaning Your Nails

Remember that dirt is often trapped under your nails. Therefore, have a good look under your nails when you wash your hands. If they are dirty, you will have to clean them. You can use a nail brush or a nail file.

© Sandra Mulvany and Brilliant Publications

Teaching Healthy Cooking and Nutrition, Book 1

This page may be photocopied by the purchasing institution only.

www.brilliantpublications.co.uk   21

Rainbow Sticks

Ingredients: Green grapes   Banana   Mangetout
Dried apricot   Mushrooms   Cherry tomatoes
Pineapple chunks

1. Wash all fruit and vegetables.

2. Peel banana.

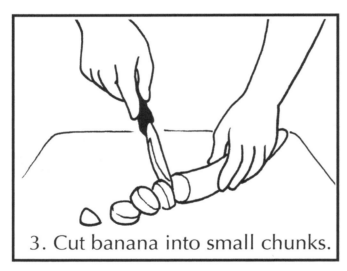

3. Cut banana into small chunks.

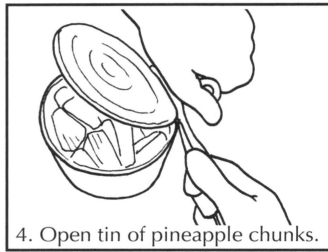

4. Open tin of pineapple chunks.

5. Drain into a sieve.

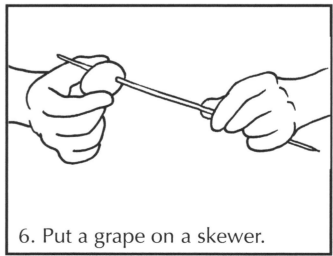

6. Put a grape on a skewer.

Rainbow Sticks (cont.)

Recipe

Equipment:

Chopping board   Tin opener   Sharp knife
Sieve   Wooden skewers

7. Then put on a cherry tomato.

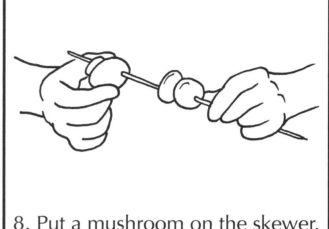

8. Put a mushroom on the skewer.

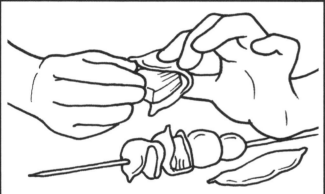

9. Fold mangetout around a
   pineapple chunk and put on.

10. Put on a banana chunk and
    a dried apricot.

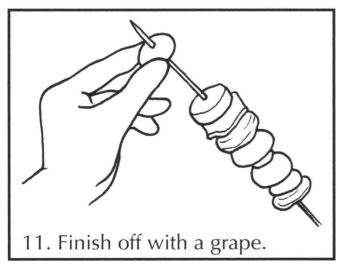

11. Finish off with a grape.

12. Make your own design.

Rainbow Sticks

Ingredients:
Green grapes
Banana
Mangetout
Dried apricot
Cherry tomatoes
Mushrooms
Pineapple chunks

Equipment:
Chopping board
Tin opener
Sharp knife
Sieve
Wooden skewers

Instructions:

1. Wash all fruit and vegetables.

2. Peel banana.

3. Cut banana into small chunks.

4. Open tin of pineapple chunks.

5. Drain into a sieve.

6. Put a grape on the skewer.

7. Then put on a cherry tomato.

8. Put a mushroom on the skewer.

9. Fold mangetout around a pineapple chunk and put on.

10. Put on a banana chunk and a dried apricot.

11. Finish off with a grape.

12. Make you own design.

Pitta Bread Filling

How to Wash Fruit and Vegetables

Skill

It is important to wash vegetables before your prepare them. It is a good idea to cut off the bits we obviously don't need before washing them. (For example, cut off the green tops of carrots before you wash them). You can put the vegetables in a colander if you want. Hold them under a cold tap and scrub them with your hands. You can also use a vegetable brush on harder vegetables.

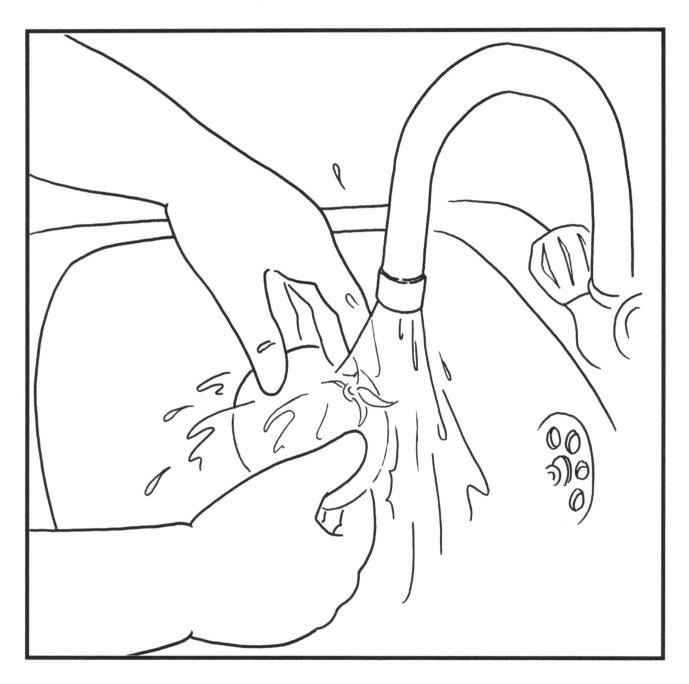

Why Wash Fruit and Vegetables?

Washing vegetables in water removes nearly all dirt, insects and bacteria. Remember that even if you grow your own vegetables, they will be full of dirt. Also remember that if you buy vegetables loose in a shop, other people may have touched them or even coughed or sneezed over them.

Advantages of an Apron

Always use an apron when you are preparing food or cooking. This is to avoid getting your clothes dirty. It also avoids any dirt from your clothes falling into the food. There are many types of aprons but the most common type slips over the head and ties around the back. Some people find it hard to tie a knot behind their back – have patience, it takes practice.

Pitta Bread Filling

Ingredients:

Pitta bread	Cucumber	Dressing	Baby corn
Iceberg lettuce	Cherry tomatoes	Mushrooms	

1. Wash the vegetables.

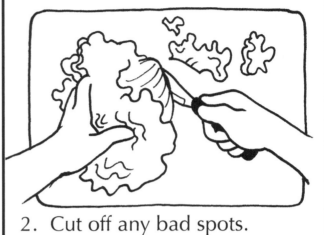

2. Cut off any bad spots.

3. Cut cucumber with Claw Method.

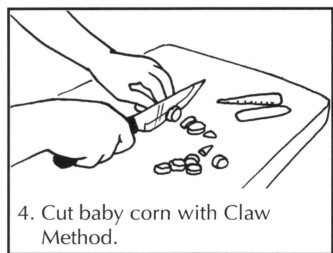

4. Cut baby corn with Claw Method.

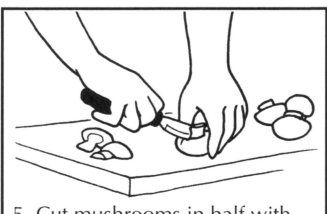

5. Cut mushrooms in half with Bridge Method.

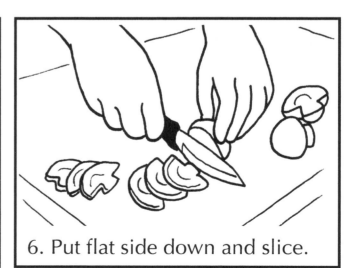

6. Put flat side down and slice.

Pitta Bread Filling (cont.)

Recipe

Equipment:

Chopping board   Sharp knife   Mixing bowl
Mixing spoon   Baking tray

7. Halve cherry tomatoes and halve again.

8. Cut the lettuce.

9. Put it all in the bowl.

10. Add dressing and mix it in.

11. Heat up pitta bread.

12. Cut a heated pitta bread open and add the salad.

Skill

Pitta Bread Filling

Ingredients:
Pitta bread
Dressing
Iceberg lettuce
Mushrooms
Cherry tomatoes
Cucumber
Baby corn

Equipment:
Chopping board
Sharp knife
Mixing bowl
Mixing spoon
Baking tray

Instructions:

1. Wash the vegetables.

2. Cut off any bad spots.

3. Cut cucumber with Claw Method.

4. Cut baby corn with Claw Method.

5. Cut mushrooms in half with Bridge Method.

6. Put flat side down and slice them.

7. Halve cherry tomatoes and halve again.

8. Cut the lettuce.

9. Put it all in a bowl.

10. Add dressing and mix it in.

11. Heat up pitta bread.

12. Cut a heated pitta bread open and add the salad.

TIP
Your teacher might heat up the pitta breads for the whole class.

Fruit Smoothie

Decorated with coloured sugar, strawberry and umbrella.

How to Remove Strawberry Stalks

If you want to take the leafy-green top off a strawberry, you have to hold onto the strawberry with one hand, whilst you twist the top gently with the other hand. If the fruit is ripe, the leafy-green top should come off easily with the white centre of the strawberry. Do it firmly, but carefully, as you do not want to crush the strawberry.

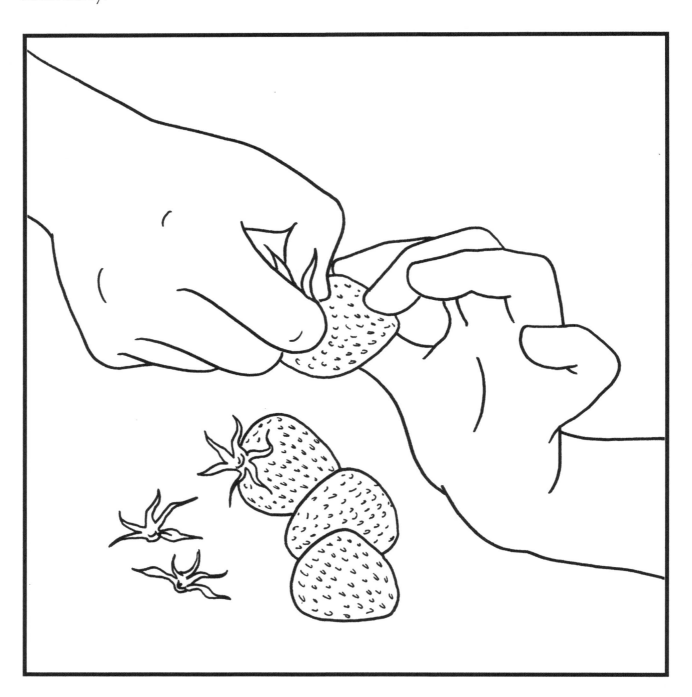

About Bananas

Bananas grow in the Tropics, which is the area centred on the equator. In particular, Ecuador, Costa Rica, the Philippines and Colombia are big exporters of bananas. Bananas grow in clusters on very tall plants that grow as high as 8 metres, with leaves as long as 3.5 metres. The bananas we find in our supermarkets are normally picked when they are still green and are transported to the UK in refrigerated ships. They are then only ripened when they arrive at their destination.

Look on packaging and labels to find out where your bananas were grown. Find the country on a globe or map of the world.

Using a Blender Safely

Be very careful when you use any type of blender. These are electrical machines with sharp parts, so you can imagine how dangerous they can be. Always make sure that the lid is tightly fitted before you start. This will avoid the food going everywhere. Also make sure that the electrical cord is in a good state of repair. When you are first learning to use a blender, you must let an adult help you. Always remember to keep electrical appliances away from water and never use them while you have wet hands.

Recipe

Fruit Smoothie

Ingredients:
4 strawberries   1 banana   1 nectarine
150ml strawberry yogurt   150ml orange juice

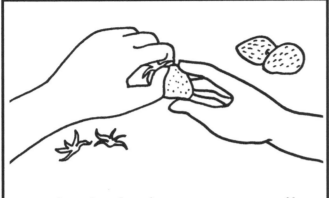

1. Take the leafy-green tops off the strawberries.

2. Wash the strawberries and the nectarine.

3. Cut the strawberries in half.

4. Peel the banana.

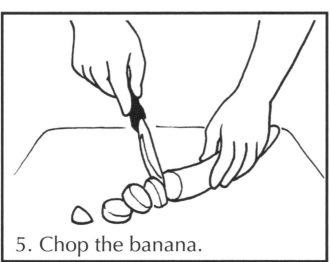

5. Chop the banana.

6. Cut the nectarine in half.

Fruit Smoothie (cont.)

Equipment:
Chopping board   Knife   Measuring jug   Blender
2 glasses

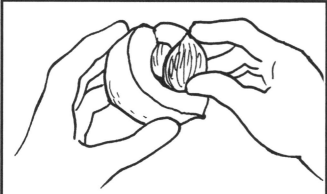

7. Take the stone out of the nectarine.

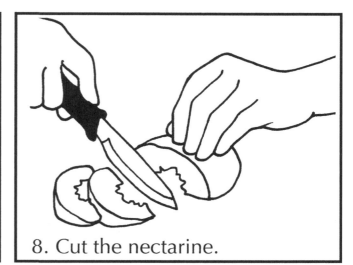

8. Cut the nectarine.

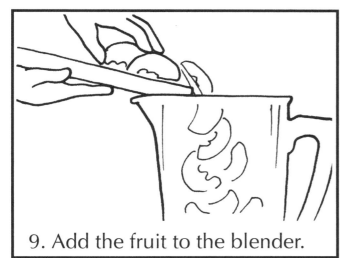

9. Add the fruit to the blender.

10. Add the yogurt to the blender.

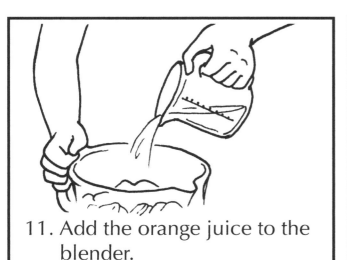

11. Add the orange juice to the blender.

12. Put the lid on and blend. Pour into the glasses.

Teaching Healthy Cooking and Nutrition, Book 1

Fruit Smoothie

Ingredients:
4 strawberries
1 banana
1 nectarine
150ml strawberry yogurt
150ml orange juice

Equipment:
Chopping board
Knife
Measuring jug
Blender
2 glasses

Instructions:

1. Take the leafy-green tops off the strawberries.

2. Wash the strawberries and the nectarine.

3. Cut the strawberries in half.

4. Peel the banana.

5. Chop the banana.

6. Cut the nectarine in half.

7. Take the stone out of the nectarine.

8. Cut the nectarine.

9. Add the fruit to the blender.

10. Add the yogurt to the blender.

11. Add the orange juice to the blender.

12. Put the lid on and blend. Pour into the glasses.

Bread Pizza

How to Spread

When you spread anything on a piece of bread, make sure that the angle of the knife is right. Support the bread with one hand and spread with the other. Make sure to spread evenly and right out to the edges.

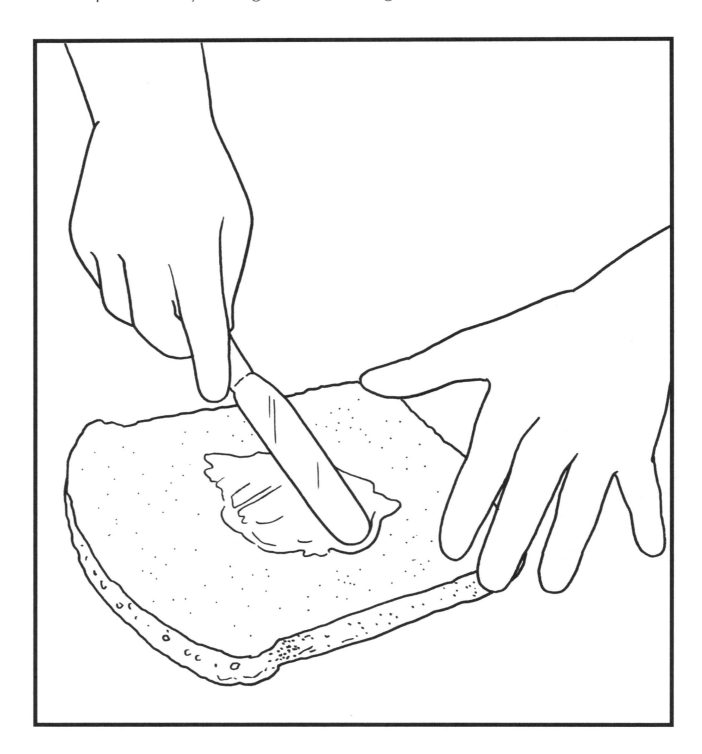

Where Does Flour Come From?

Theory

The flour we use in baking normally comes from wheat. Wheat is a type of cereal that farmers grow in their fields in the summer. It looks golden when it is ripe for harvesting. After harvesting, the grains get milled and this is how flour is produced.

There are many varieties of flour: wholemeal, brown and white being the main types. Wholemeal flour is where the whole grain is used. Brown flour uses about 85% of the kernel, removing some of the outer part (known as bran). White flour only uses the central part, or endosperm, removing most of the wheat grain's nutrients altogether.

Reasons to Tie Back our Hair

Health & Safety

Always put your hair up if you have long hair. It is unhygienic to have your long hair loose in the kitchen. Your hair can also get caught in appliances or even catch fire, not to mention loose hair falling out in the food.

© Sandra Mulvany and Brilliant Publications

This page may be photocopied by the purchasing institution only.

Teaching Healthy Cooking and Nutrition, Book 1

www.brilliantpublications.co.uk   **39**

Recipe

Bread Pizza

Ingredients:
Slice of brown bread
2 spring onions

2–3 tbsp tomato purée
2 slices of ham   50g cheese

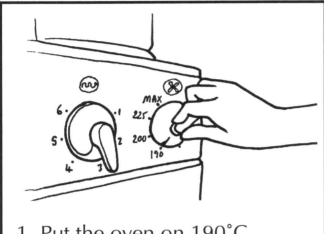

1. Put the oven on 190°C.

2. Get all your equipment out.

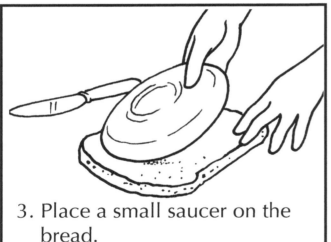

3. Place a small saucer on the bread.

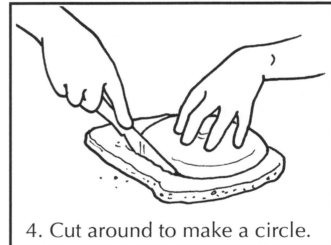

4. Cut around to make a circle.

5. Spread purée on the circle of bread.

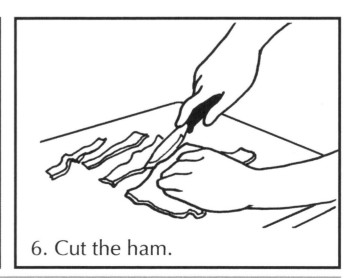

6. Cut the ham.

Bread Pizza (cont.)

Equipment:

Small saucer	Butter knife	Chopping board	Scales
Sharp knife	Baking tray	Grater	Tablespoon

7. Put the ham on the bread.

8. Chop the spring onion.

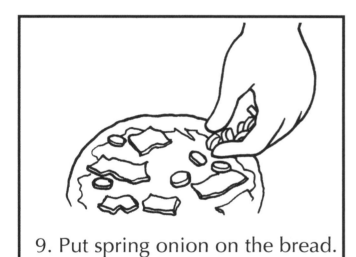

9. Put spring onion on the bread.

10. Weigh and grate the cheese.

11. Sprinkle the cheese on.

12. Bake for 10–15 minutes.

Bread Pizza

Ingredients:
Slice of brown bread
2–3 tbsp tomato purée
2 spring onion
2 slices of ham
50g cheese

Equipment:
Small saucer
Butter knife
Chopping board
Sharp knife
Baking tray
Grater
Tablespoon
Scales

Instructions:

1.   Put the oven on 190°C.

2.   Get all your equipment out.

3.   Place a small saucer on the bread.

4.   Cut around to make a circle.

5.   Spread purée on the circle of bread.

6.   Cut the ham.

7.   Put the ham on the bread.

8.   Chop the spring onion.

9.   Put spring onion on the bread.

10.   Weigh and grate the cheese.

11.   Sprinkle the cheese on.

12.   Bake for 10–15 minutes.

Afternoon Tea Bread

Skill

How to Weigh Ingredients

You have to know your numbers to be able to weigh accurately. There are many types of weighing scales: electronic scales, scales with a dial and old-fashioned scales with balance and weights. They all require different skills. Remember that if you are using electronic scales, you must zero them first and make sure that you are measuring in grams (and not ounces). Also remember that you cannot take the bowl on and off if you are using electronic scales.

Types of Flour – Which is Healthier?

Our baking flour is normally made from wheat. A grain of wheat consists of the bran, the wheatgerm and the endosperm. White flour is made by grinding only the endosperm. Brown flour is made by grinding about 85% of the grain. Wholemeal flour is made by grinding the whole grain, including all the bran and the wheatgerm which contain both fibre and vitamins B and E. This is why foods made using wholemeal flour are much healthier for us.

Reasons to Avoid Dangly Sleeves

You must never wear dangly sleeves when you are working in the kitchen. Not only will they get dirty, but the sleeves can also easily get caught in appliances or even catch fire.

Afternoon Tea Bread

Ingredients: 75g wholemeal flour   1 tsp baking powder
50g plain flour   25g margarine   1 tsp cinnamon
2 tsp sugar   ½ egg   75ml milk

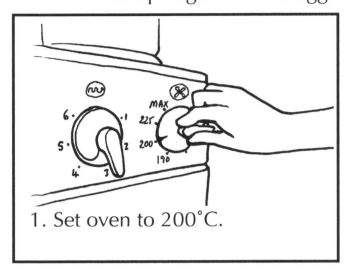

1. Set oven to 200°C.

2. Weigh out the flours and margarine.

3. Combine the flours and rub in the margarine.

4. Add the sugar, cinnamon and baking powder.

5. Crack the egg into a cup.

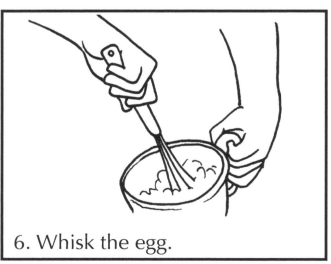

6. Whisk the egg.

Afternoon Tea Bread (cont.)

Recipe

Equipment: Scales   Mixing bowl   Teaspoon
Mixing spoon   Whisk/fork   Cup   Measuring jug
Flour dredger   Rolling pin   Baking tray

7. Add the milk and ½ of the egg to the bowl.

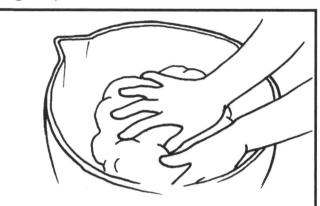

8. Stir to mix together. Use hands to form a big ball.

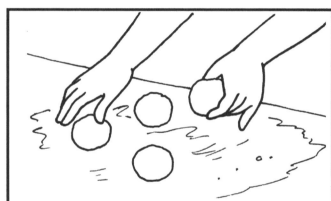

9. Divide into 4 balls of dough on a floured surface.

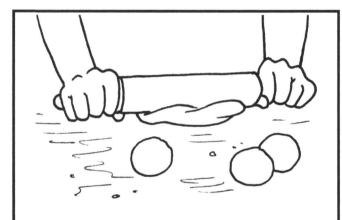

10. Roll out each ball of dough.

11. Put on a greased baking tray.

12. Bake for 10–15 minutes.

Afternoon Tea Bread

You Will Need:
75g wholemeal flour
50g plain flour
25g margarine
1 tsp baking powder
2 tsp sugar
1 tsp cinnamon
½ egg
75ml milk

Equipment:
Scales
Mixing bowl
Teaspoon
Mixing spoon
Egg whisk
Cup
Measuring jug
Baking tray
Rolling pin
Flour dredger

Instructions:

1.   Set oven to 200°C.

2.   Weigh out the flours and margarine.

3.   Combine the flours and rub in the margarine.

4.   Add the sugar, cinnamon and baking powder.

5.   Crack the egg into a cup.

6.   Whisk the egg.

7.   Add the milk and ½ of the egg to the bowl.

8.   Stir to mix together. Use hands to form a big ball.

9.   Divide into 4 balls of dough on a floured surface.

10.   Roll out each ball of dough.

11.   Put on a greased baking tray.

12.   Bake for 10–15 minutes.

TIP
Share 1 egg between 2 sets of partners after you have whisked it.

Couscous Salad

How to Sprinkle

When you sprinkle a stock cube, you simply have to rub and squeeze the cube between your fingers and let it sprinkle. Be careful when you have to sprinkle it into boiling water, as the steam can burn you. If possible, allow the saucepan to cool down slightly before you sprinkle or alternatively, sprinkle the cube into your hand and then add it carefully, but quickly, to the hot water.

What is Couscous?

Couscous is made from crushed wheat. For centuries it has been one of the main foods eaten in North African countries, namely Morocco, Algeria and Tunisia. Its bland flavour means that it tastes good with lots of different kinds of ingredients: spices, meats, vegetables or fruit. Traditionally, couscous is made by a lengthy process of rolling, rubbing, sieving, moistening and drying the wheat. Nowadays, you can just buy it ready-made at the supermarket.

Reasons to Close Cupboard Doors

Always close cupboard doors after you. This is because open cupboard doors are a hazard in the kitchen. You and other people could easily fall over an open low cupboard door or bang your head on it if it's a higher door.

© Sandra Mulvany and Brilliant Publications

This page may be photocopied by the purchasing institution only.

Teaching Healthy Cooking and Nutrition, Book 1

www.brilliantpublications.co.uk 51

Couscous Salad

Ingredients:

100g couscous	1 tsp fresh coriander	
200ml water	1 stock cube	4 cherry tomatoes
1 tbsp sultanas	4 sugar snap peas	4 baby sweet corn

1. Wash the vegetables.

2. Add 200ml water to a saucepan.

3. Bring the water to the boil.

4. Sprinkle in the stock cube.

5. Add the couscous.

6. Put a lid on and take off the hob.

Couscous Salad (cont.)

Recipe

Equipment:

Scales	Measuring jug	Saucepan and lid
Mixing spoon	Sharp knife	Chopping board

7. Leave couscous for 10 minutes.

8. Cut the tomatoes and sugar snap peas.

9. Cut the baby sweet corn.

10. Add it all to the couscous and mix.

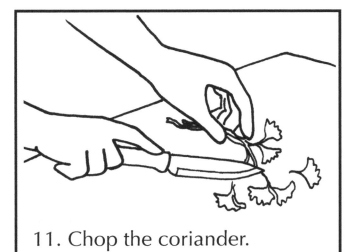

11. Chop the coriander.

12. Add the sultanas and coriander. Mix and serve.

Couscous Salad

Ingredients:
100g couscous
4 baby sweet corn
4 cherry tomatoes
4 sugar snap peas

200ml water
1 stock cube
1 tbsp sultanas
1 tsp fresh coriander

Equipment:
Scales
Measuring jug
Saucepan and lid
Mixing spoon
Sharp knife
Chopping board

Instructions:

1.   Wash the vegetables.

2.   Add 200ml water to a saucepan.

3.   Bring the water to the boil.

4.   Sprinkle in the stock cube.

5.   Add the couscous.

6.   Put a lid on and take off the hob.

7.   Leave couscous for 10 minutes.

8.   Cut the tomatoes and sugar snap peas.

9.   Cut the baby sweet corn.

10.   Add it all to the couscous and mix.

11.   Chop the coriander.

12.   Add the sultanas and coriander. Mix and serve.

Irish Soda Bread

© Sandra Mulvany and Brilliant Publications

This page may be photocopied by the purchasing institution only.

Teaching Healthy Cooking and Nutrition, Book 1

www.brilliantpublications.co.uk   **55**

How to Turn the Oven on

You need to know your numbers in order to turn on an oven. An electric oven is easier to put on than a gas oven. With some electric ovens, you need to switch them on at the wall first. Then you need to find the right control knob and turn it to the correct temperature. The number you want may just be shown as a small dot between two other numbers. On some gas ovens, you must press the ignition to get a spark. Keep holding down the ignition button and turn the control knob. Do not let go of the ignition button until you have a flame.

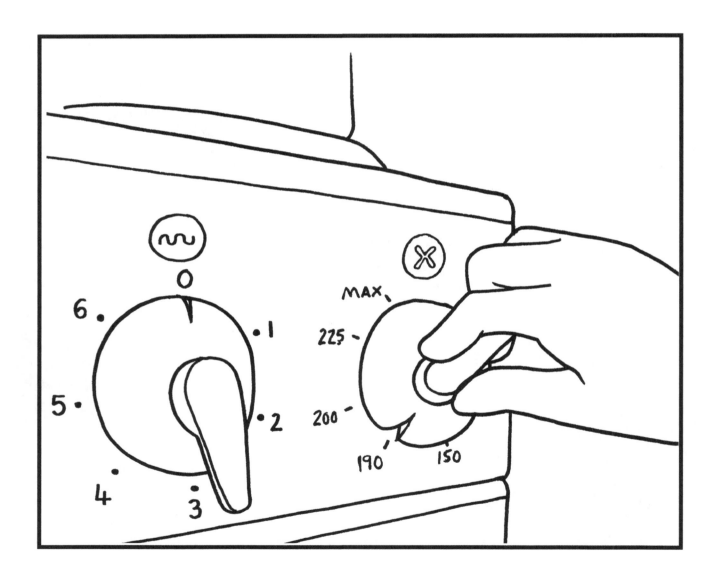

When is the Oven Hot Enough?

An oven takes a while to heat up to the right temperature. Most ovens have an indicator light next to the control knobs. This light will come on when you turn on the oven. It will go off when the temperature you chose has been reached.

Gas Ovens Are Dangerous

Be VERY careful with gas ovens. You need a flame to burn off the gas. If there is no flame and the gas is coming out, the entire room will fill with gas. This is very dangerous. At the slightest spark, a room or house full of gas will explode with obvious consequences. Close gas oven doors carefully, otherwise the rush of air caused by the closing will put out the flame. Be aware of any smell of gas. If you discover that gas is coming out, you must turn the oven off straight away, open the windows and leave the room. Never try to ignite the oven with gas in the room.

If you should enter a room and smell gas, NEVER turn on the light switch as this can create a spark which can ignite the gas and cause an explosion.

Irish Soda Bread

Ingredients: 100g wholemeal flour   100g plain flour
1 tsp bicarbonate of soda   1 tsp baking powder   ½ egg
1 tbsp brown sugar   150ml natural yogurt

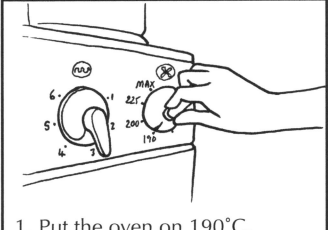

1. Put the oven on 190°C.

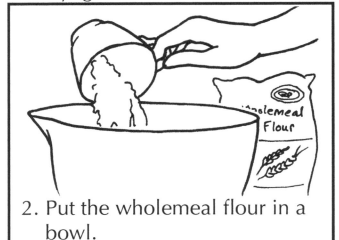

2. Put the wholemeal flour in a bowl.

3. Add the plain flour and mix.

4. Add the baking powder and mix.

5. Add the bicarbonate of soda and mix.

6. Add the sugar and mix.

Irish Soda Bread (cont.)

Equipment: Scales   Flour dredger
Measuring jug   Mixing bowl   Measuring spoons   Cup
Knife   Whisk/fork   Mixing spoon   Baking tray

7. Crack an egg into a cup and whisk.

8. Add half the egg to the yogurt.

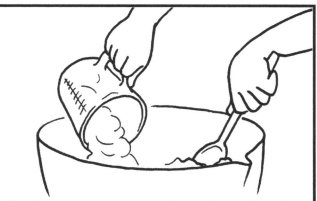

9. Add this to the bowl and mix to form a dough.

10. Lightly knead on a floured surface and shape into 4 rolls.

11. Put on a baking tray and cut a cross in the top.

12. Bake for 10–15 minutes.

Irish Soda Bread

Ingredients:
100g wholemeal flour
100g plain flour
1 tsp bicarbonate of soda
1 tsp baking powder
½ egg
1 tbsp brown sugar
150ml natural yogurt

Equipment:
Scales
Measuring jug
Cup
Whisk/fork
Baking tray
Baking tray

Flour dredger
Mixing bowl
Knife
Mixing spoon
Measuring spoons

Instructions:

1.   Put the oven on 190°C.

2.   Put the wholemeal flour in a bowl.

3.   Add the plain flour and mix.

4.   Add the baking powder and mix.

5.   Add the bicarbonate of soda and mix.

6.   Add the sugar and mix.

7.   Crack an egg into a cup and whisk.

8.   Add half the egg to the yogurt.

9.   Add this to the bowl and mix to form a dough.

10.   Lightly knead it on a floured surface and shape into 4 rolls.

11.   Put on a baking tray and cut a cross in the top.

12.   Bake for 10–15 minutes.

TIP
Share 1 egg between 2 sets of partners after you have whisked it.

Pizza

How to Roll out

Make sure that your dough isn't too sticky. If it is, add a bit more flour. Sprinkle a little flour onto the table and roll your rolling pin in it. Shape the dough into a ball and gently roll it out. Turn the dough over and keep turning it around so that you are rolling it into a circle. If the dough begins to stick, sprinkle a little more flour from the flour dredger over the rolling pin or over the dough.

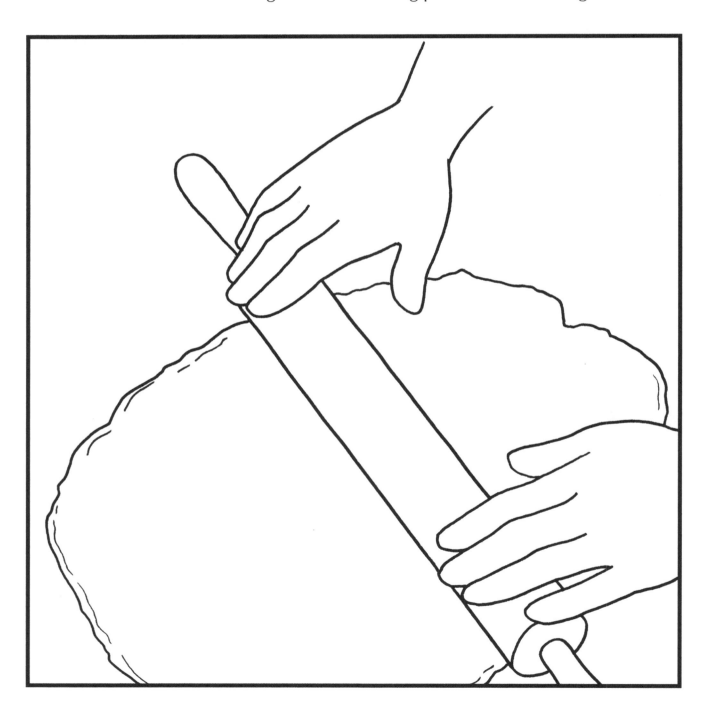

About Carbohydrates

Carbohydrates are found in wheat, oats, potatoes, rice or any food made from these, such as bread. These are starchy carbohydrates and they give you slow-releasing energy for work and warmth.

Sugar is another type of carbohydrate. It gives you a quick rush of energy, but it doesn't last. Of course, sugar isn't good for your teeth, so stick with starchy carbohydrates.

Realizing Knives are Sharp

Do not forget that knives are very sharp. If you touch the sharp blade, you can cut yourself. Always point the sharp blade down towards the table. You can always put a mark on the handle to show which side is safe and which side is sharp.

If you have to carry a sharp knife, you must be especially careful. Hold it firmly in your hand with the blade pointing straight down.

Pizza

Ingredients:

Pepperoni	100g self-raising flour	Sweet corn
2–3 tbsp tomato purée	25g margarine	50ml milk
	½ tsp mixed herbs	75g cheese

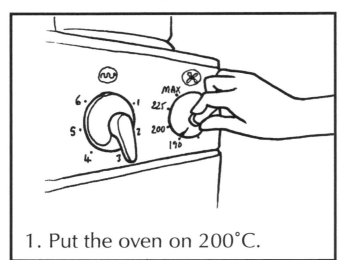

1. Put the oven on 200°C.

2. Sieve flour into bowl.

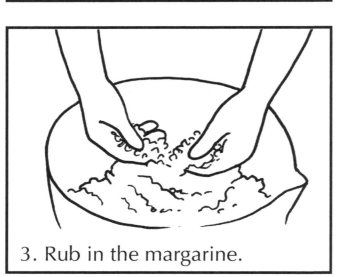

3. Rub in the margarine.

4. Add milk to form a dough.

5. Roll out to a circle on a floured surface.

6. Put dough on a greased baking tray.

Pizza (cont.)

Equipment: Sharp knife Mixing bowl Scales Sieve
Flour dredger Teaspoon Mixing spoon Chopping board
Grater Measuring jug Rolling pin Baking tray

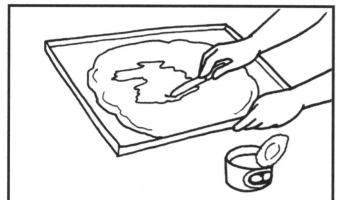

7. Spread tomato purée over the pizza.

8. Sprinkle on some sweet corn.

9. Cut the pepperoni and put it on the pizza.

10. Grate the cheese and sprinkle over.

11. Sprinkle over the herbs.

12. Bake for 15–20 minutes.

Pizza

Ingredients:
100g self-raising flour
Sweet corn
2–3 tbsp tomato purée
Pepperoni
25g margarine
50ml milk
½ tsp mixed herbs
75g cheese

Equipment:
Sharp knife   Mixing bowl
Teaspoon   Scales
Mixing spoon   Sieve
Flour dredger   Chopping board
Grater   Measuring jug
Rolling pin   Baking tray

Instructions:

1. Put oven on 200°C.

2. Sieve flour into bowl.

3. Rub in the margarine.

4. Add milk to form a dough.

5. Roll out to a circle on a floured surface.

6. Put dough on a greased baking tray.

7. Spread tomato purée over the pizza.

8. Sprinkle on some sweet corn.

9. Cut the pepperoni and put it on the pizza.

10. Grate the cheese and sprinkle over.

11. Sprinkle over the herbs.

12. Bake for 15–20 minutes.

Welsh Rarebit

How to Use a Grill

It can be dangerous using a grill. It gets very hot and it is normally placed inside an oven, making it awkward to get to. Normally, you also need to have the oven door open to use the grill, creating another hazard. Remember to pay attention when you are using the grill. A grill can take a while to heat up. When it is hot, slide the grill tray in carefully and bend down to keep an eye on it. Do not stand too close to it, as you may get burnt by spitting fat or food fragments.

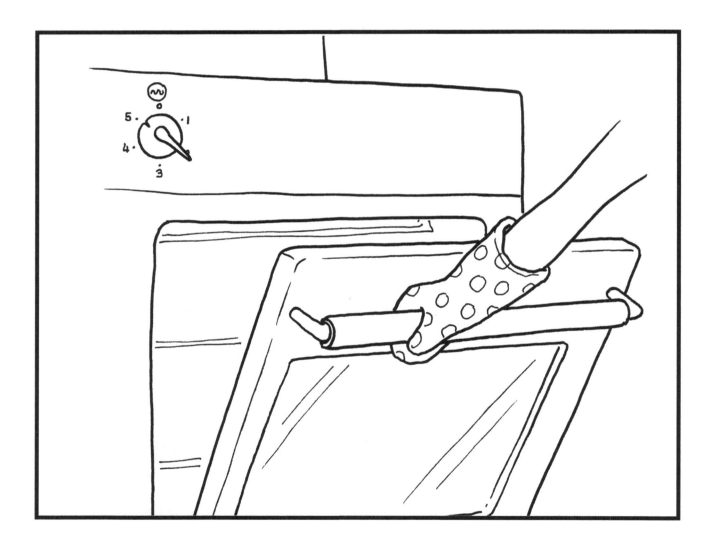

About Calcium

Calcium is a mineral found in milk. Therefore, calcium is found in anything made from milk, such as cheese and yogurt. Calcium is good for bones and teeth. Calcium is especially important for growing children, pregnant women and older people with weak bones. Calcium is also found in dark green leafy vegetables, such as kale.

Reasons to Avoid Running Around

Never run in a kitchen. There are many hazards in a kitchen and you would be putting yourself and others in danger. If you are not careful and bump into someone, food can be spilled, burning someone if it is hot or making the floor slippery and hazardous.

Welsh Rarebit

Ingredients:

1 tomato	2 slices of brown bread	2 tbsp milk
Butter to spread	75g Cheddar cheese	1 tsp mustard
	Pinch of salt and pepper	

1. Grate the cheese.

2. Put it in a bowl.

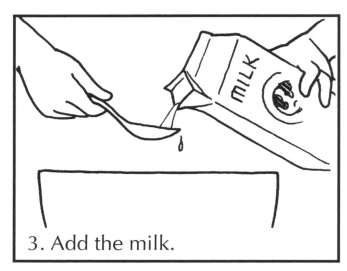

3. Add the milk.

4. Add the mustard, salt and pepper.

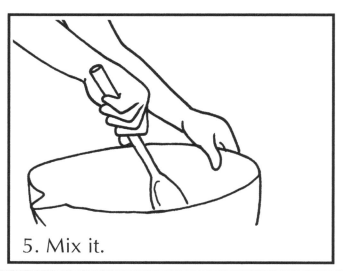

5. Mix it.

6. Slice a tomato.

Welsh Rarebit (cont.)

Equipment:

Grater	Chopping board	Mixing spoon
Sharp knife	Measuring spoons	Knife Mixing bowl Toaster

Recipe

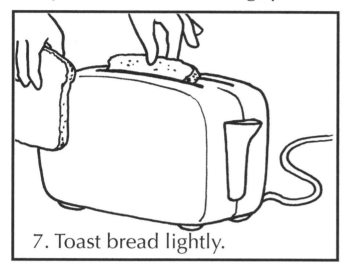

7. Toast bread lightly.

8. Spread butter over the toast.

9. Spread the filling over the toast.

10. Put under a hot grill until brown and bubbly.

11. Put a slice of tomato on top.

12. Reheat and serve.

Teaching Healthy Cooking and Nutrition, Book 1

Welsh Rarebit

Ingredients:
2 slices of brown bread
2 tbsp milk
1 tomato
75g Cheddar cheese
1 tsp mustard
Butter to spread
Pinch of salt and pepper

Equipment:
Grater
Chopping board
Measuring spoons
Mixing spoon
Sharp knife
Mixing bowl
Knife
Toaster

Instructions:

1. Grate the cheese.

2. Put it in a bowl.

3. Add the milk.

4. Add the mustard, salt and pepper.

5. Mix it.

6. Slice a tomato.

7. Toast bread lightly.

8. Spread butter over the toast.

9. Spread the filling over the toast.

10. Put under a hot grill until brown and bubbly.

11. Put a slice of tomato on top.

12. Reheat and serve.

Chinese Noodle Soup

How to Squeeze a Lemon

You can squeeze a lemon using your hand, but it is much easier if you use a lemon squeezer. There are many types of lemon squeezers and all will generally catch any pips. Cut the lemon in half and place the fleshy part of the fruit over the tip of the squeezer, press down firmly and turn the fruit back and forth until all the juice has been extracted. Oranges, grapefruits and limes can all be squeezed this way.

How Are Noodles Made?

Noodles are a good source of carbohydrates. There are many types. Noodles are often used in Chinese dishes and most are made from wheat flour, water and egg. Usually, the dough is either cut to the desired width and dried or pushed through a mechanical press and dried.

Remember that pasta and noodles are made, but potatoes and rice are grown.

Stirring Hot Liquid Safely

Hot liquid can burn, so if you are stirring liquids such as soup or gravy, do it carefully and slowly. Hold the saucepan handle with your other hand, but make sure you keep the handle away from the hob. Do not lean over the saucepan, as the hot steam can burn you too.

Chinese Noodle Soup

Ingredients: Spring onions   Courgette   Mushrooms
1 tsp ginger   Stock cubes   600ml water   Vegetable oil
½ lime   1 tbsp soy sauce   1 portion noodles

1. Wash spring onions, courgette and mushrooms.

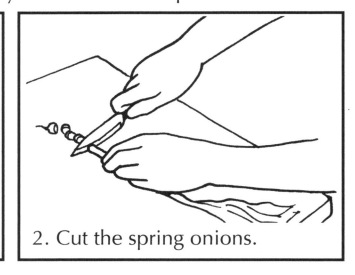

2. Cut the spring onions.

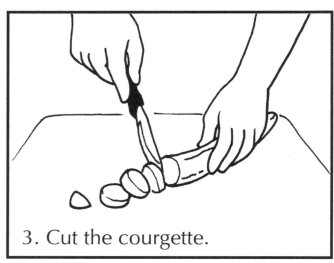

3. Cut the courgette.

4. Slice the mushrooms.

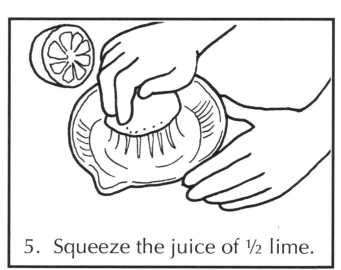

5. Squeeze the juice of ½ lime.

6. Heat a little oil in a saucepan.

Chinese Noodle Soup (cont.)

Recipe

Equipment:

Chopping board   Sharp knife   Measuring jug

Lemon squeezer   Mixing spoon   Saucepan   Measuring Spoons

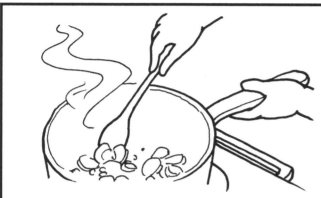

7. Lightly fry spring onions, courgette and mushrooms.

8. Add the water.

9. Add soy sauce, stock cubes and ginger.

10. Add the lime juice.

11. Bring to the boil and simmer for 2–3 minutes.

12. Add the noodles and simmer for another 5 minutes.

Teaching Healthy Cooking and Nutrition, Book 1

Chinese Noodle Soup

Ingredients:
Spring onions
Courgette
Mushrooms
1 tsp ginger
Stock cubes
600ml water
Vegetable oil
½ lime
Noodles (1 portion)
1 tbsp soy sauce

Equipment:
Chopping board
Sharp knife
Measuring jug
Measuring spoons
Lemon squeezer
Mixing spoon
Saucepan

Instructions:

1.   Wash spring onions, courgette and mushrooms.

2.   Chop the spring onions.

3.   Chop the courgette.

4.   Slice the mushrooms.

5.   Squeeze the juice of ½ a lime.

6.   Heat a little oil in a saucepan.

7.   Lightly fry spring onions, courgette and mushrooms.

8.   Add the water.

9.   Add soy sauce, stock cubes and ginger.

10. Add the lime juice.

11. Bring to the boil and simmer for 2–3 minutes.

12. Add the noodles and simmer for another 5 minutes.

TIP
Share 1 lime between 2 sets of partners.

Danish Frikadeller

How to Turn Food Over

Be very careful when you turn any food over in a hot frying pan. The fat can easily spit/splash-back and burn you. Make sure that you do not lean over the pan as this will increase your risk of getting burnt. There are several ways you can turn food: using a turner, a pair of safety tongs or even by using two dessertspoons. When you turn using a turner, do it very carefully and don't flip the food suddenly. If you drop the food, the fat can spit and burn your hands, arms and/or face. Safety tongs may be easier to use, but aren't suitable for all foods, for example, a fried egg might burst. Using the two spoons may be more difficult for some people, but again will avoid splash-back of fat. Whichever method you choose to adopt, remember to hold the pan handle.

Utensils

Lean or Fat Meat – Which is Better?

Meat has fat in it, and sometimes meat has a lot of fat in it. Too much fat is not good for the heart, and it can also lead to obesity. The fat looks white before it has been cooked. Therefore, you can see the fat that meat has in it. "Lean meat" means meat that is low in fat, and this is less bad for you. Therefore, be aware of the fat content in meat. When you buy minced pork, a fatty meat, buy the kind with the least fat in it.

Reasons for Keeping Your Hands Clean

It is not always enough to just wash your hands before you start cooking. Sometimes you have to wash them at regular intervals. This may be because you have touched something that may have bacteria on it, or it may be because you need clean working hands. In this recipe, you will have to wash your hands after you have touched the raw meat.

Recipe

Danish Frikadeller

Ingredients: 250g lean minced pork   150ml milk
Margarine   Pinch of pepper   50g plain flour
½ egg   1 small onion   (serve on rye bread)

1. Put the meat in a bowl.

2. Mix in the pepper.

3. Chop the onion finely, add and mix.

4. Crack the egg in a cup. Whisk it and add half of it.

5. Add the milk and mix.

6. Add the flour and mix.

Danish Frikadeller (cont.)

Recipe

Equipment: Mixing bowl   Whisk/fork   Measuring jug
Sharp knife   Frying pan   Cup   Chopping board
Scales   Turner   Mixing spoon   Dessertspoon

7. Shape the mixture into balls using a dessertspoon.

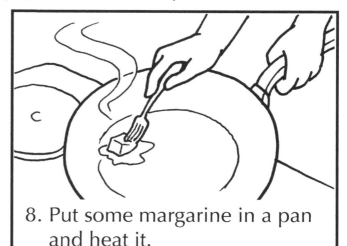

8. Put some margarine in a pan and heat it.

9. Put the frikadeller in the pan and fry for 2 minutes.

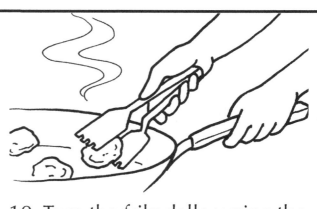

10. Turn the frikadeller using the turner.

11. Fry for another 2 minutes.

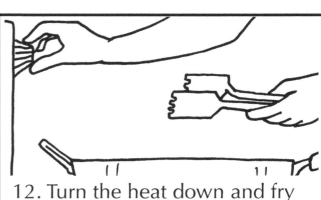

12. Turn the heat down and fry for another 4 minutes on each side.

Skill

Danish Frikadeller

Ingredients:
250g lean minced pork
Margarine
Pinch of pepper
½ egg
50g plain flour
150ml milk
1 small onion
(You can serve it on rye bread)

Equipment:
Mixing bowl
Measuring jug
Frying pan
Scales
Turner
Dessertspoon

Whisk/fork
Sharp knife
Cup
Chopping board
Mixing spoon

Instructions:

1.   Put the meat in a bowl.

2.   Mix in the pepper.

3.   Chop the onion finely, add and mix.

4.   Crack the egg in a cup. Whisk it and add half of it.

5.   Add the milk and mix.

6.   Add the flour and mix.

7.   Shape the mixture into balls using a dessertspoon.

8.   Put some margarine in a pan and heat it.

9.   Put the frikadeller in the pan and fry for 2 minutes.

10. Turn the frikadeller using the turner.

11. Fry for another 2 minutes.

12. Turn the heat down and fry for another
     4 minutes on each side.

TIP
Share 1 egg
between 2 pairs.
Divide the egg
after you have
whisked it.

What can you remember? (1)

Do this quiz after lesson 6.

1. What does food do for us?

   It gives us nutrients It gives us the giggles It does our homework

2. What should you always do before you start cooking?

   Ring your best friend Wash your hands Put on the radio

3. Where do we get vitamin C from?

   In the classroom In fruit and vegetables At a football match

4. Can human beings store vitamin C in their bodies?

   No Yes Only in the summer

5. Why do we wash fruit and vegetables?

   To make them smell better To clean their ears To wash off dirt and bacteria

6. Where do bananas grow?

   In London In the Tropics On the Moon

7. Where does flour come from?

   It comes from wheat It comes in a bag It grows on trees

8. Which letter should normally be displayed on electric scales?

   ml oz g

9. Why is wholemeal flour healthier than white?

   It goes to the gym It uses the whole grains It rides a bike

10. Should you wear dangly sleeves whilst cooking?

    No Only if they are pretty Yes

Name _____ Date _____ Score _____

What Can You Remember? (2)

Do this quiz after lesson 12.

1. What should you do if you see an open cupboard door?
   Run away   Close it   Ignore it

2. Should you communicate about what you are doing whilst cooking?
   No, never say a thing   Yes, always   Only if it is
                            communicate   your best friend

3. Why can gas ovens be dangerous?
   They like to kick people   They can fill a room   They have a
                              with gas   black belt

4. What are carbohydrates good for?
   For sleeping   For driving cars   For energy

5. What should you do if the dough becomes sticky when you roll it out?
   Add flour   Start crying   Leave the kitchen

6. What is Welsh Rarebit?
   A Welsh bunny rabbit   A type of cheese on   A rare insect
                            toast   bite in Wales

7. What is calcium good for?
   For the blood   For the lungs   For teeth and bones

8. Should you run in a kitchen?
   Yes, as fast as you can   No   Only if you are fit

9. How are noodles made?
   From wheat and egg   From sugar   From recycled paper

10. Why should we use lean meat?
    It can lean against the   It is easier to fry   There is less fat in it
    wall

Name _____ Date _____ Score _____

Certificate of Achievement

Teaching Healthy Cooking and Nutrition, Book 1

Name

_____

Is Able to

Cut Food

Put Food on a Skewer

Wash Vegetables

Remove
Strawberry stalks

Spread Using a
Knife

Weigh
Ingredients

Sprinkle

Turn Oven on

Roll out Pastry

Use a Grill

Squeeze Lemons

Turn Food Over

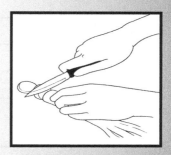

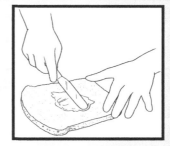

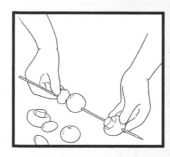

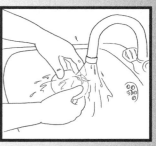

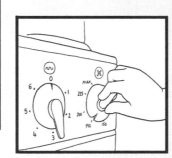

Allergy/lifestyle/religious considerations

The chart below lists possible substitutions that can be made (where possible) for children with common allergies/intolerances and/or lifestyle/religious considerations. It is not exhaustive and it is important to check with parents prior to doing any cooking activities.

Recipe	Possible substitutions
Fruit Salad	None
Rainbow Sticks	None
Pitta Bread Filling	Gluten free pitta bread can be bought in many supermarkets, for children with gluten/wheat allergies.
Fruit Smoothie	None
Bread Pizza	For children with wheat or gluten allergies, gluten free bread may be used. The ham may be omitted for vegetarians or children who don't eat ham for religious reasons.
Afternoon Tea Bread	This recipe is not suitable for children with gluten or wheat allergies. (Alternative gluten free recipes can be found on the Internet.)
Couscous Salad	Gluten free couscous can be used for children who are allergic to gluten.
Irish Soda Bread	This recipe is not suitable for children with gluten, wheat and/or egg allergies. (Alternative gluten free/egg free recipes can be found on the Internet.)
Pizza	For children will gluten/flour allergies, gluten free self-raising flour can be substituted, but the end result will be much crumblier. Non-dairy cheese and milk can be purchased in large supermarkets for children who are lactose intolerant. The pepperoni may be omitted for vegetarians or children who don't eat ham for religious reasons.
Welsh Rarebit	Gluten-free bread may be used for children who have gluten/flour allergies. Non-dairy hard cheese and milk may be purchased in most large supermarkets for children who are lactose intolerant. Note: calcium is often added to non-dairy milks.

Recipe	Possible substitutions
Chinese Noodle Soup	Rice noodles can be used for children with gluten/wheat allergies. If anyone has a soy allergy, then the soy sauce should be omitted. A teaspoon of balsamic vinegar (and possibly some salt) could be added instead.
Danish Frikadeller	This recipe is not suitable for vegetarians. Minced beef could be used instead of minced pork for pupils who don't eat pork due to religious reasons. Gluten free flour can be used instead of plain flour for children with gluten/wheat allergies. Gluten free rye bread is available in some stores (alternative gluten free bread could be substituted).